GREEK ISLAND MYTHS

LESBOS (MYTILENE)
SAPPHO AND ORPHEUS

JILL DUDLEY

PUT IT IN YOUR POCKET SERIES
ORPINGTON PUBLISHERS

Published by
Orpington Publishers

Cover design and origination by
Creeds, Bridport, Dorset
01308 423411

Printed and bound in the UK by
Creeds

© Jill Dudley 2017

ISBN: 978-0-9934890-8-2

LESBOS (MYTILENE)
SAPPHO AND ORPHEUS

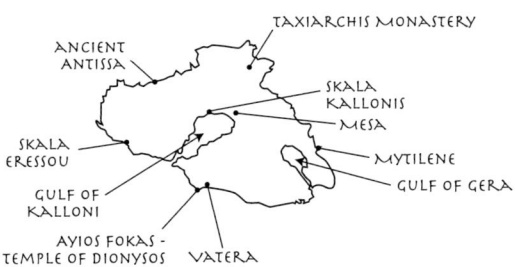

The island of Lesbos in the north-east of the Aegean is also known as Mytilene which is the name of its port. The island has its own charm, you might almost describe it as lyrical, aptly so because it is the birthplace of Sappho, the great seventh century B.C. lyric poetess. A very ancient legend also links Orpheus to the island – Orpheus the divine singer and player of the lyre, who sang so beautifully that the mountains bowed down to hear, the fish leapt from the sea to listen, and animals would draw near.

The port of Mytilene is horse-shoe shaped. When you look across the bay from its southern curve you see the ancient acropolis which in antiquity was a small islet with a narrow channel that separated it from the main island. It was there that the city was first built, but over the years the channel silted up and the expanding population spread across to the main island.

On the west coast of Lesbos is Skala Eressou where Sappho was born and lived till she was fifteen. Close by is an acropolis where, it is said, she used to sit and sing, accompanying herself on a lyre, and watching for her merchant brother's return from his frequent visits to Egypt. When her father died, she was taken by her mother to Mytilene where she founded a school for girls. She loved all things beautiful which often included her young pupils with whom she had lesbian relationships – the English word 'lesbian' comes from the island's name and from Sappho's love of young girls.

Sappho mixed with her fellow aristocrats, and taught her girls poetry, singing and the lyre. She and her pupils performed at symposiums, weddings or at special functions and religious festivals. She married and had a daughter called Cleis. Her husband, however, was unfaithful and the marriage ended. She took part in politics but, as an anarchist, was eventually sent into exile, living either in Sicily or Cyprus. Because, as some believe, she had a horror of growing old, or, as others think, because she fell hopelessly in love with a ferryman and was rejected by him, she leapt off a cliff to her death. But her poems were left for the world to treasure, and her name lives on. In fact, her genius was such that she influenced the greatest minds down the centuries, and Plato called her the tenth Muse.

She worshipped Aphrodite, goddess of love, and beseeched her divine assistance in her love affairs. An hour's drive from Mytilene to Kalloni, a signpost indicates Mesa to the right where there is an archaeological site, until recently said to be an ancient temple of Aphrodite. Recent archaeologists, however, have discovered worship there of Zeus, Hera and Dionysos. With Sappho in mind, it is tempting to go along with traditional belief, and to imagine her coming to beseech the goddess of love in Mesa's tranquil, rural setting.

The island also has ties with Orpheus, the legendary poet and divine singer and mystic, who came from Thrace on mainland Greece. He was believed to be the son of Apollo and Calliope, one of the nine Muses. He was said to have been one of the Argonauts, and it was his divine singing that helped get the boat, the Argo, past the Siren Voices. These were fabulous creatures whose singing was so hypnotic that all mariners who heard them were lured to their destruction. Orpheus, however, outdid them with the beauty of his voice, and the Argonauts passed safely by.

The name of Orpheus today is usually remembered when linked to his beloved wife Eurydice who, newly married to Orpheus, died of a snake bite. Orpheus was overwhelmed with grief. By singing and playing his lyre he charmed both Charon (the ferryman who rowed the dead across the river Styx), and also Cerberus (the multiple-headed dog who guarded the entrance to the underworld). His singing so entranced the god Hades himself and his wife Persephone, that they allowed Eurydice to return with Orpheus to the upper world on condition that Orpheus led the way and never looked back at his young bride. Tragically, in the joy of reclaiming his wife, Orpheus forgot the injunction and, as they neared the light, he glanced back to check that she was following, and Eurydice was at once doomed to remain in Hades for eternity.

Orpheus was so inconsolable that he shunned company from then on, especially the company of women. He had been an ardent worshipper of Dionysos whose followers were mainly women known as Maenads. These Maenads would go into ecstatic trances which gave them super-human strength, enabling them to tear apart live bulls which they then devoured – a strange sort of worship and ritual. The female Maenads resented being ignored by Orpheus and one day, instead of attacking a bull, they set upon Orpheus, tore him limb from limb and decapitated him. However, his head, still singing, floated from mainland Greece over the Aegean sea to Lesbos, to Ancient Antissa, an isolated small promontory in the north-west of the island. His head floated up a nearby river, then settled in a cave a few kilometres from Ancient Antissa. Tradition has it that it had oracular powers

and the islanders began to consult it, receiving answers to their questions, until Apollo grew angry as he felt his son was usurping his role as prophet, so he put a stop to it.

Lesbos is within easy reach of Turkey, and sided with Troy during the Trojan War. Consequently it was invaded by the Greeks. In the south of the island, on the way to the archaeological site of an ancient temple of Dionysos eight kilometres west of Vatera, there is a deep stone-built well, known as the Well of Achilles. Achilles* was the famous Greek warrior who fell out with King Agamemnon* because he demanded for himself Achilles' beautiful and beloved slave-girl named Briseis. It is interesting that local tradition has it that Briseis came originally from the nearby village of Brissa, and many of the local girls there are named Briseis after the slave-girl. Farmers in the vicinity have turned up ancient arrow heads and helmets from the Trojan War period. Also, when the nearby harbour of Agios Fokas was being deepened, similar artefacts were dredged up.

There is also a remarkable Christian warrior legend on Lesbos. This concerns St. Michael the Archangel. In the north-east of Lesbos is the Taxiarchis Monastery which possesses a miracle-working icon made from human blood dating from the tenth century. The icon was the consequence of a Saracen pirate raid. The story goes that early one morning when the monks were at their dawn prayers, pirates attacked and slaughtered all the monks except for one young novice who climbed through a window to the roof. He was, however, spotted and the pirates were about to kill him when a roar was heard, the roof turned into heavy seas, and on the crest of the waves stood a magnificent warrior. The pirates were terror-stricken, and the young novice fainted. When he came to he beseeched an icon for help and guidance, and found himself fashioning a new icon using clay mixed with blood taken from the slaughtered monks around him. An invisible power guided his hand as he created this new icon of the Archangel Michael.

The icon today stands on an ornately carved and inlaid stand with an arched canopy, and the dark made-with-clay-and-human-blood face of St. Michael is surrounded by embossed silver. The Archangel wears a crown, and he has large archangel wings, and bears a sword.

St. Michael is petitioned by soldiers in particular. It is said that sometimes the eyes of the Archangel are seen to shed tears, or he is seen to smile, or, if someone unworthy approaches, he will be driven back by his divine power. Below the icon are pairs of metal shoes; the shoes are presented to the Archangel by a petitioner and, at some later date, the soles will be examined to see if they are worn down; this is sometimes the case which means the Archangel has been actively engaged in searching for a solution to the petitioner's problem.

Lesbos is an island whose landscape varies from rugged gorges to rolling low mountains. Its land is well tended with vast olive groves and small allotments. Two large inland gulfs penetrate the island to the south. It has its own uniqueness, and the word lyrical fits it well. Visitors come away from Lesbos feeling both uplifted and bewitched, touched by a certain magic which the island possesses.

* Denotes a separate booklet on the subject.

SOME GODS BORN OF ZEUS

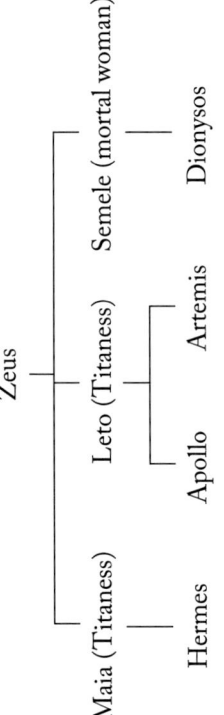

FAMILY TREE OF THE TITANS, GODS AND GODDESSES

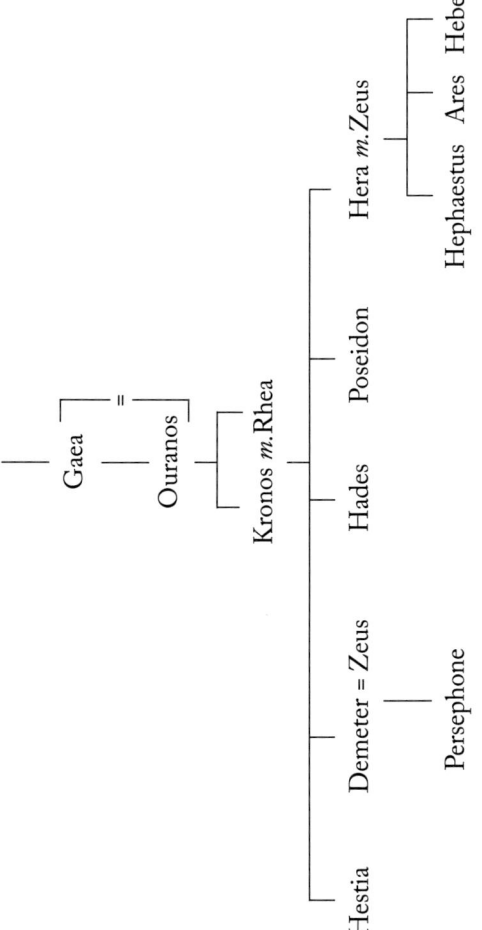

GLOSSARY OF GODS AND GODDESSES

APHRODITE – Goddess of love. There are two stories of her birth. One that she was the daughter of Zeus and Dione. The other that she arose fully grown from the sea at Paphos in Cyprus. She was married to the lame god Hephaestus.

APOLLO – Son of Zeus and the Titaness Leto. He was twin brother of Artemis, and god of medicine, music, archery ad prophecy.

ARTEMIS – Daughter of Zeus and the Titaness Leto, and twin sister of Apollo. She was goddess of wild life and defender of the very young.

DIONYSOS – Son of Zeus and the mortal woman Semele. He was god of wine and drama. Women who worshipped him celebrated his rites with song and dance, and often went into a state of ecstasy and frenzy becoming capable of tearing apart wild beasts which they devoured; they were known as the Maenads.

HADES – God of the underworld.

HERA – Wife of Zeus, and goddess of women and marriage.

MNEMOSYNE – A Titaness. She was the mother by Zeus of the Muses.

MUSES – The nine daughters of Zeus and the Titaness Mnemosyne. They were the goddesses of the fine arts, music, literature, and later covered such other subjects as history, philosophy and astronomy.

PERSEPHONE – Daughter of Zeus and Demeter. She was abducted by Hades and dragged screaming to his kingdom in the underworld. With Zeus' intervention she was allowed back up to her mother for eight months of the year and returned to Hades for the other four.

TITANS – The offspring of Ouranos (often spelt Uranus, the heavens) and Gaea (the earth). There were said to be twelve of them, six sons and six daughters. Kronos was one of the sons, and Rhea one of the daughters. These two had six children amongst whom were Hera, Hades and Zeus.

ZEUS – Son of the Titans Kronos and Rhea. He was god of the heavens, and supreme god of the ancient world having deposed his father.

More from the
Put it in your Pocket series

Trojan War
The Judgement of Paris
Helen
King Agamemnon
Achilles
The Wooden Horse
Odysseus

Sacred Sites
Athens – The Acropolis
Corinth – St. Paul and the Goddess of Love
Delphi – The Oracle of Apollo
Eleusis – Demeter and Kore
Epidaurus – Centre of Healing
Olympia – The Olympic Games

ALSO BY JILL DUDLEY

YE GODS! (TRAVELS IN GREECE)
YE GODS! II (MORE TRAVELS IN GREECE)
LAP OF THE GODS (TRAVELS IN CRETE
AND THE AEGEAN ISLANDS)